All About Food

By Michael Teitelbaum
Illustrated by Joe Ewers and John Carrozza
Cover design by Brad Marks

A Muppet Press Book

Hi-ho! Kermit the Frog here! Did you ever wonder where your food comes from? Well, stick with me and Robin and you'll find out!

What is food?

Food is everything we eat to give us energy. Just as cars and trucks need gas to make them go, our bodies need food to make *us* go. Food also keeps us healthy and strong.

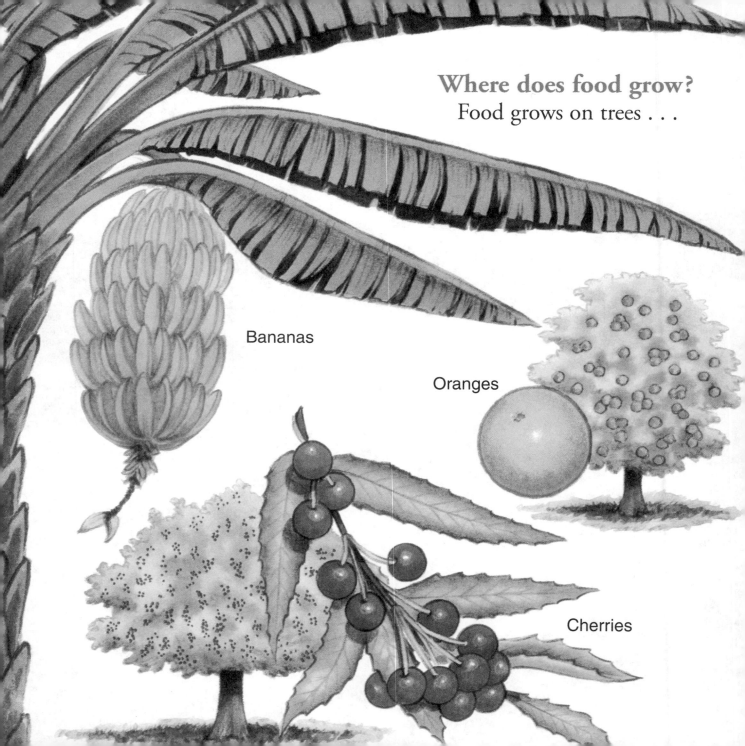

Where does food grow?
Food grows on trees . . .

Bananas

Oranges

Cherries

on bushes and vines . . .

Peppers

Tomatoes

Beans

Pumpkins

and under the ground.

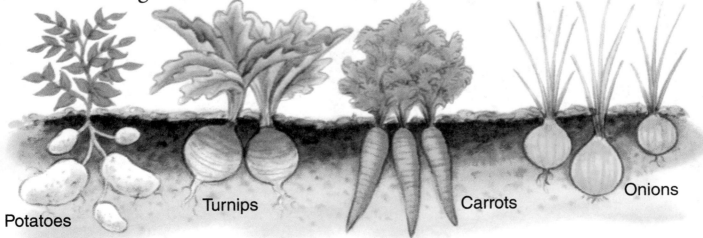

Potatoes

Turnips

Carrots

Onions

Does cheese grow on trees?

No, cheese is made from milk, which comes from cows. Cows are milked two or three times a day. Each day the milk is taken to a dairy.

To make cheese, dairy workers add special ingredients to the milk and then stir it. The milk gets thick and lumpy and after a while it becomes cheese.

Many other things can be made from milk, like ice cream, yogurt, and butter.

Ice cream

YOGURT

Cheese

Butter

If butter comes from milk, does peanut butter come from milk, too?

Peanut butter is made from peanuts, which grow in the ground. After the farmer picks the peanuts, he takes the shells off and roasts the nuts in a big oven.

Peanuts

The roasted nuts are put into a grinder, and they turn into peanut butter.

Do you know how to make a peanut butter and jelly sandwich? First take two slices of your favorite kind of bread. Then spread peanut butter on one slice and jelly on the other. Put the two sticky sides together, and you've got a peanut butter and jelly sandwich! Mmm-mm!

How do you make jam?

It's easy to make jam. I'm making strawberry jam right now. First I'll boil the strawberries. Then I'll add some sugar. I'll cook the jam until it gets nice and thick, let it cool, and pour it into jars.

You can make jam out of almost any fruit you want, like peaches, blueberries, and grapes. And each kind is delicious!

Where does bread come from?

Bread is made from grains like wheat, rye, and oats.

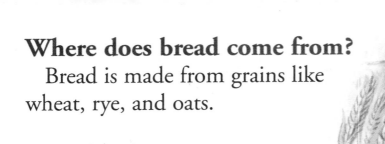

Wheat

The grain is ground into a fine powder called flour.

The flour is then mixed with yeast, water, and salt to make a dough. The yeast makes the dough rise, or get bigger.

When the dough is baked in an oven, it turns into bread!

What other foods can be made from grains?
A lot of yummy foods can be made from grains!

Spaghetti

Cookies

Rice

RICE

PANCAKE MIX

BEST SYRUP

Pancakes

Cold Cereal

CORN FLAKES

Hot Cereal

Biscuits

Where does maple syrup come from?

All trees have a liquid inside them called sap. The sap of sugar maple trees is very sweet. We can collect sap from these trees in the late winter and early spring. But we can't take too much or it will harm the trees. When the sap is boiled for a long time, it turns into syrup. It takes about 40 cups of sap to make just one cup of syrup!

Does honey come from a honey tree?

No, it's made by honeybees. First the bees collect a sweet liquid called nectar from flowers.

The nectar turns into honey inside the bees' bodies. The bees store the honey in special honeycombs that they build inside their hives.

Where do eggs come from?

Eggs come from chickens. You can scramble eggs, fry them, make omelettes with them, bake them—and even decorate them!

How do raisins grow?

Raisins don't grow at all! They are grapes that have been left to dry in the sun. The drier they get, the sweeter they are.

Raisins are yummy! Why can't you just eat them all the time?

To be healthy, you need to eat many kinds of food every day: fruits, vegetables, grains, and foods that have a lot of protein. Proteins include chicken, fish, cheese, nuts, or beans. These foods help build strong bones and muscles and give you more energy.

Vegetables contain vitamins that help your body grow strong and stay healthy. Spinach and carrots have vitamin A, which helps you see better. Broccoli and green peppers have vitamin C, which keeps your gums and teeth in good shape.

All this talk about food can sure make you hungry. What's for lunch?

Pizza!

Pizza is made from many different kinds of food from many different places! The pizza crust is made from flour, which is ground from wheat. The cheese is made from milk, which comes from cows. The tomato sauce is made from tomatoes, which grow on vines.

Your turn!

Here's an easy recipe you can try at home—and now you know where all the ingredients come from. When you're done, you'll have a treat that's good for breakfast, lunch, or a snack!

Yogurt Delight

You will need:
small bowl
small container of plain yogurt
spoonful of honey
handful of raisins
banana
cold cereal

1. Ask a grown-up to slice the banana for you.
2. Pour the yogurt, honey, and raisins into the bowl. Add the banana slices. Use a spoon to mix them together.
3. Top this delicious treat with your favorite cold cereal, right from the box!